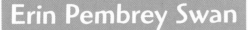

Erin Pembrey Swan

Primates

From Howler Monkeys to Humans

Franklin Watts - A Division of Grolier Publishing
New York • London • Hong Kong • Sydney • Danbury, Connecticut

For Michelle, because she loved the little critters

Photographs ©: Ellis Nature Photography: 1, 5 bottom left, 6, 39; Minden Pictures: cover, 37 (Mitsuaki Iwago), 5 top left, 5 top right, 7, 17, 21, 29, 33, 35, 41 (Frans Lanting); National Geographic: 44 (Robert M. Campbell), 42, 43; Photo Researchers: 31 (Alan D. Carey), 23, 25 (Tim Davis), 5 bottom right (Jeff Lepore), 15 (Tom McHugh), 4 (Will & Deni McIntyre), 27 (Gary Retherford), 13, 19 (Jany Sauvanet).

Illustrations by Jose Gonzales and Steve Savage.

Visit Franklin Watts on the Internet at:
http://publishing.grolier.com

Library of Congress Cataloging-in-Publication Data

Swan, Erin Pembrey
    Primates: From howler monkeys to humans / Erin Pembrey Swan.
    p. cm. — (Animals in order)
    Includes bibliographical references and index.
    Summary: Discusses the order of the animal kingdom known as primates and describes the members of fifteen different species that are found in the Americas, Africa, Madagascar, and Asia.
    ISBN 0-531-11487-2 (lib.bdg.)   0-531-15921-3 (pbk.)
    1. Primates—Juvenile literature. [1. Primates.] I. Title. II. Series.
QL737.P9S796   1998
599.8—dc21   97-29567
                                         CIP
                                         AC

Contents

What Is a Primate?

What do you think of when you look at your mother and father? Your brothers and sisters? Your friends?

You probably think of them as people, or maybe as humans. Both of these are true. But they also belong to a larger group, called an *order*. The order that you and all other people belong to is called the primates.

Humans are not the only primates in the world. There are many other animals in this order. The most obvious ones are monkeys and apes, but the list does not end there, either.

All but one of the animals shown on the next page is a primate. Can you guess which one is *not* a primate?

Gorilla

Tarsier

Lemur

Otter

Traits of a Primate

Did you choose the otter? You were right! How can you tell it is not a primate?

Most primates have five separate fingers on each hand. Look at your own hand. Notice how your thumb is set opposite the rest of your fingers. Most primates' fingers are arranged the same way. This helps them grab, hold, and use objects.

Just as you would hold a pencil, a chimpanzee would hold a stick and use it to pry open termite mounds and catch the tiny insects inside. The hands of primates are also useful for grabbing branches and vines. This is important because many primates sleep and look for food in trees.

Primates have eyes on the front of their faces, rather than on the sides. This is helpful for primates that live in forests. *3-D vision* makes it easier to move from tree to tree.

Primates usually have only one or two babies at a time. They are dedicated parents, and raise their children to adulthood. Because the adults are around to protect their young, they don't need to have as many babies as some other types of animals.

Most primates eat only plants. However, many eat both plants and other animals, such as insects or grubs.

Except for humans, almost all primates live in only four places—Central and South America, Africa, Asia, and the island of Madagascar.

The Order of Living Things

A tiger has more in common with a house cat than with a daisy. A scorpion is more like a butterfly than a jellyfish. Scientists arrange living things into groups based on how they look and how they act. A tiger and a house cat belong to the same group, but a daisy belongs to a different group.

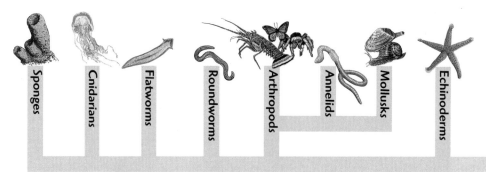

Sponges · Cnidarians · Flatworms · Roundworms · Arthropods · Annelids · Mollusks · Echinoderms

Animals

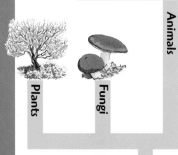

Plants · Fungi

Protists

Monerans

All living things can be placed in one of five groups called *kingdoms:* the plant kingdom, the animal kingdom, the fungus kingdom, the moneran kingdom, or the protist kingdom. You can probably name many of the creatures in the plant and animal kingdoms. The fungus kingdom includes mushrooms, yeasts, and molds. The moneran and protist kingdoms contain thousands of living things that are too small to see without a microscope.

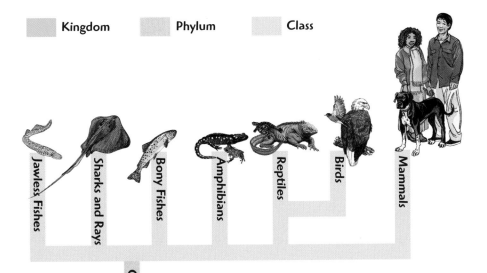

Kingdom Phylum Class

Jawless Fishes
Sharks and Rays
Bony Fishes
Amphibians
Reptiles
Birds
Mammals

Chordates

Because there are millions and millions of living things on Earth, some of the members of one kingdom may not seem all that similar. The animal kingdom includes creatures as different as tarantulas and trout, jellyfish and jaguars, salamanders and sparrows, elephants and earthworms.

To show that an elephant is more like a jaguar than an earthworm, scientists further separate the creatures in each kingdom into more specific groups. The animal kingdom can be divided into nine *phyla*. Humans belong to the chordate phylum. All chordates have a backbone.

Each phylum can be subdivided into many *classes*. Humans, mice, and elephants all belong to the mammal class. Each class can be further divided into *orders*; orders into *families*, families into *genera*, and genera into *species*. All of the members of a species are very similar.

9

How Primates Fit In

You can probably guess that the primates belong to the animal kingdom. They have much more in common with bears and bats than with maple trees and morning glories.

Primates belong to the chordate phylum. Almost all chordates have a backbone and a skeleton. Can you think of other chordates? Examples include elephants, mice, snakes, birds, fish, and whales.

The chordate phylum can be divided into a number of classes. Primates belong to the mammal class. Elephants, mice, dogs, and cats are all mammals.

There are seventeen different orders of mammals. The primates make up one of these orders. The name "primates" has the same root as the word "primary," which means first. Scientists believe that primates are the most highly developed order of living things, and humans are considered to be the most highly evolved species. This is because we have large brains that allow us to think and reason.

The primates can be divided into a number of different families and genera. There are 233 species of primates. You will learn more about some of the primates in this book.

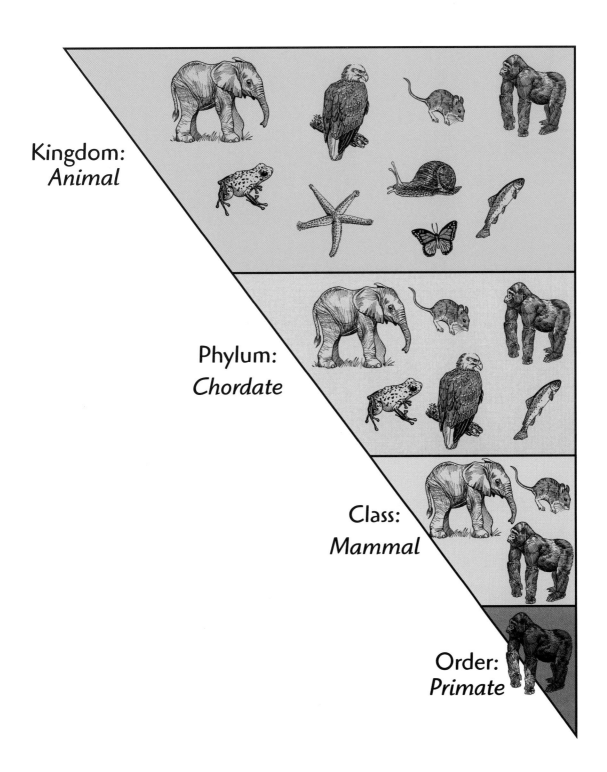

Kingdom: *Animal*

Phylum: *Chordate*

Class: *Mammal*

Order: *Primate*

Howler Monkeys

FAMILY: Cebidae

COMMON EXAMPLE: Red howler

GENUS AND SPECIES: *Alouatta seniculus*

SIZE: 22 inches (56 cm); tail 25 inches (64 cm)

Imagine a tropical rain forest at dawn—the thick, moist air, the huge leaves overhead, the sounds of animals slowly waking up. Suddenly, a loud howling cry splits the air, drowning out the songs of birds. What could it be?

The male howler monkey of South America, which is about the size of a large dog, has a special way of keeping out unwanted neighbors. The bone at the base of a howler's tongue—the *hyoid bone*—is unusually wide. The howler's lower jaw is wide, too. This allows the monkey to use its throat like a sort of trumpet.

Howler monkeys use their special trumpet to make a sound somewhere between a howl, a hoot, and a screech. Heard at dawn and again at dusk, this sound tells other howler monkeys, "Keep away! This is my home!" Sometimes, neighboring *troops* of howlers have a sort of vocal battle. The chorus may last for hours.

Howler monkeys are very social. Most live in troops with ten to twenty members. They spend their mornings searching for and eating fruit, leaves, and young shoots. In the afternoon, howler monkeys usually rest.

Tamarins

FAMILY: Callitrichidae
COMMON EXAMPLE: Emperor tamarin
GENUS AND SPECIES: *Saguinus imperator*
SIZE: 9 inches (23 cm); tail 14 inches (36 cm)

Who's king of the Amazon rain forest? The long moustaches of the emperor tamarin are fit for royalty.

Tamarins live together in small groups. The females usually give birth to twins. Male tamarins play an important role in caring for the babies. The males play with the babies and often carry them around on their backs. Only when it is feeding time are the males willing to let the the babies' mother take over.

Like most people, tamarins sleep at night and are awake during the day. They spend the day climbing among the trees. Although they cannot grab and hold branches with their tails, they are excellent climbers. Except for their big toes, they have claws on all their fingers and toes. These claws help them scamper along branches without falling off. If they do fall, they can drop a long way without getting hurt.

The tamarin calls to other animals in the forest with its shrill voice. Its calls may warn of danger or announce the location of food.

Spider Monkeys

FAMILY: Cebidae
COMMON EXAMPLE: Black spider monkey
GENUS AND SPECIES: *Ateles paniscus*
SIZE: 20 inches (51 cm); tail 27 inches (69 cm)

Is that a huge, furry spider in the tree? No, it's just a black spider monkey hanging from a branch by its tail. But its long, thin arms and legs certainly make it look like a spider.

Spider monkeys are excellent climbers. They jump from branch to branch, using both hands and feet. Their *prehensile* tails act as a fifth hand, holding onto branches and searching cracks for food. A spider monkey can leap up to 30 feet (9 m). That's as far as five tall men lying in a row!

Spider monkeys make their homes in the trees, as high as 100 feet (31 m) above the ground. That's where they sleep, play, and raise their children. They move lower only to gather food, such as fruit and nuts.

Spider monkeys live in small friendly groups. During the day, they stay within calling distance of each other. If they feel threatened, the monkeys group together to protect each other. Some groups consists of a female and her babies. Others have only males. Still others include a male, his female mates, and their children.

If you are ever in the South American rain forest, look up and you may see spider monkeys hanging from the highest branches.

Squirrel Monkeys
FAMILY: Cebidae
COMMON EXAMPLE: Common squirrel monkey
GENUS AND SPECIES: *Saimiri sciureus*
SIZE: 10 to 16 inches (25.4 to 40.6 cm);
   tail 16 inches (41 cm)

Who's making all that noise? A group of squirrel monkeys gathers high in the treetops to chatter, bicker, and chase one another. They are the liveliest and most common primates of South America, so their presence is no secret to anyone walking underneath their tree-top homes.

Squirrel monkeys are known for their intelligence. They are also extremely energetic and social. Although most spider monkeys live in groups with 10 to 35 members, some groups have more than 300 monkeys. They nestle togther at night to sleep and often fight for the warmest spot in the middle of the furry group. When day comes, they scatter to hunt for fruit, insects, eggs, and—best of all—a tasty tree frog or two.

One tiny, furry squirrel monkey is born at a time, like a human baby. Until it can move about on its own, each bright-eyed baby is carried on the back of a willing adult squirrel monkey. The parents take turns giving piggy-back rides. If both parents are busy, a female relative often babysits.

Squirrel monkeys get their name from their small size and their

squirrel-like agility. They can leap easily from tree to tree and scamper up and down the trunks.

Next time you hear a couple of squirrels chattering noisily at each other, think how much noise 100 squirrel monkeys must make!

19

Gorillas

FAMILY: Pongidae
COMMON EXAMPLE: Gorilla
GENUS AND SPECIES: *Gorilla gorilla*
SIZE: 48 to 72 inches (122 to 183 cm)

After a long morning of gathering fruit, roots, and bamboo shoots to eat, a group of mountain gorillas needs to rest. Two females quietly groom each other. Using their thumbs and forefingers, they pick leaves, twigs, and lice out of each other's thick fur. An older male, called a silverback because he has silver-colored fur on his back, sits nearby to watch for danger.

Unlike the fabled King Kong, these gentle primates are not dangerous unless they are attacked. If this happens, the silverback will stand up on his back legs, hoot, throw plants around, and beat his chest. If the enemy has not run away, the silverback lets out a huge roar. The gorillas rarely hurt an intruder.

Female gorillas usually give birth to one baby at a time. At the age of 4 months, the baby gorilla begins to travel on its mother's back. When it's big enough, the young gorilla begins to play with other gorillas. They climb trees, swing on branches, and slide down tree trunks. They have even been seen playing a game like tug-of-war. What fun to be a young gorilla growing up in the African jungle!

Chimpanzees

FAMILY: Pongidae
COMMON EXAMPLE: Common chimpanzee
GENUS AND SPECIES: *Pan troglodytes*
SIZE: 24 to 48 inches (61 to 122 cm)

Mmm! A chimpanzee munches termites off a stick. After wetting it with spit, the chimpanzee poked the stick into a termite nest. When the chimpanzee pulled the stick out, it was covered with tasty termites. What a smart way to get lunch!

Chimpanzees are famous for their creativity. Like humans, they use objects as tools. They use banana skins to clean their fur. They even use leaves to collect and drink rainwater. In captivity, chimpanzees have even been known to draw and paint abstract pictures!

Of all primates, chimpanzees are most like humans. To share their feelings they smile, bare their teeth, pucker their lips, or press their lips together. They also use a variety of sounds to communicate. Adult chimpanzees often kiss, hold hands, and comfort one another.

Like human children, young chimpanzees grow up slowly. When a chimpanzee is very young, its mother carries it in her arms. When the young chimpanzee is larger, it rides on her back.

Young chimpanzees love to play. They climb trees, wrestle, and play with anything they can find. Curiosity starts early with chimpanzees!

Baboons

FAMILY: Cercopithecidae
COMMON EXAMPLE: Sacred baboon
GENUS AND SPECIES: *Papio hamadryas*
SIZE: 27 inches (69 cm); tail 19 inches (48 cm)

Watch out for sacred baboons! They can hold their own against dogs, leopards, and even humans. With their big manes and long fangs, they can look as scary as any lion.

These baboons are not always so terrifying. They are dangerous only when they are attacked. And, in fact, the more peaceful females may not defend themselves at all. Females do not have manes, and they are smaller and browner than the silver-colored males.

Sacred baboons spend most of their time looking for food in the deserts and open plains of Africa. They may walk up to 12 miles (22 km) a day in search of plant roots and fruits, lizards, scorpions, insects, and ostrich eggs.

All baboons live in large groups called troops. There may be as many as 300 baboons in a troop. During the day, the troop breaks up into smaller groups (30 to 90 individuals) to hunt. At night, all of the members of the troop sleep together.

Young baboons are raised by their mothers. Like most other primates, when a baboon is born, it clings to its mother's chest. As it grows older, the young baboon begins to ride on its mother's back. It's like getting a piggyback ride all the time!

Bushbabies

FAMILY: Lorisidae
COMMON EXAMPLE: Senegal bushbaby
GENUS AND SPECIES: *Galago senegalensis*
SIZE: 6 inches (15 cm); tail 9 inches (23 cm)

A Senegal bushbaby pounces on a praying mantis. Got it! The mantis makes a tasty meal for this small primate.

Bushbabies, or galagos, as they are often called, live in forests or open shrubby areas. During the day, they sleep in nests made of leaves and twigs. The nests are located in hollow trees or in tree forks.

At sunset, bushbabies wake up and begin their nightly search for food. Senegal bushbabies follow familiar pathways to their favorite feeding places. Their big eyes and excellent hearing help them find prey in the dark.

After a long night of pouncing on insects and drinking nectar from the large flowers of the baobab tree, bushbabies look for cozy trees to spend the day in. Before sleeping, they fold their large ears up like fans.

Bushbabies can spring from tree to tree, as if they were flying. On the ground, they hop like tiny kangaroos. Senegal bushbabies can leap up to 15 feet (4.5 m). When they're scared, bushbabies either jump to safety or remain completely still, looking like lumps of moss.

Lemurs

FAMILY: Lemuridae
COMMON EXAMPLE: Ring-tailed lemur
GENUS AND SPECIES: *Lemur cattaa*
SIZE: 16 inches (41 cm); tail 23 inches (58 cm)

Is that a raccoon? No, it's a ring-tailed lemur. The long, ringed tails and dark eye patches of ring-tailed lemurs might make you think that they are cousins of the raccoons you may have seen in your backyard. Actually, they are much more closely related to you than they are to racoons.

Lemurs live together in large groups. Most prefer areas with plenty of trees for them to climb around in, but not the ring-tailed lemurs. Some ring-tailed lemurs live on rocky plains where there are few trees.

They spend most of their time on the ground. All morning they hunt for food. In the afternoon, they rest—sunbathing and grooming each other. Luckily, there's always a lemur willing to pick lice from another's fur or share a tasty bird's egg plucked fresh from the nest.

Baby lemurs are born one or sometimes two at a time. To cling to its mother's chest, a baby lemur wraps its legs around its mother's waist and grasps her shoulders with its hands. Young lemurs always drag on the ground. When the young lemur is a bit older, it rides on its mother's back.

Aye-ayes

FAMILY: Daubentoniidae

EXAMPLE: Aye-aye

GENUS AND SPECIES: *Daubentonia madagascariensis*

SIZE: 14 to 17 inches (36 to 43 cm); tail 22 to 24 inches (56 to 61 cm)

Tap tap tap! An aye-aye taps a log with its long middle finger. It stops to listen to the faint sounds its tapping has produced. What's that? With its large front teeth, the aye-aye tears eagerly into the log and then digs out the insects inside with its long, slender fingers. What a great snack!

Aye-ayes live in the rain forests of northern Madagascar. They sleep the day away in ball-shaped nests made of leaves and branches. Each nest is tucked snugly into the fork of a tree. At sundown, the aye-aye crawls of its nest through a hole in the side. It is ready for a night of adventure.

The aye-aye has very special hands. They are perfect for finding food in hard-to-reach places. Its middle fingers are longer than the rest. They look like dry, bent twigs. They are good for spearing insects hiding inside dead logs or poking into crevices that might contain food. Aye-ayes also groom their thick fur and bushy tails with these two fingers.

Sadly, you are not likely to see an aye-aye. There are very few of them. In addition, they sleep during the day. Even if you went to Madagascar, you might not see one. They are so small and quiet that even if you were looking right at one, you might not notice it.

Lorises

FAMILY: Lorisidae
COMMON EXAMPLE: Slow loris
GENUS AND SPECIES: *Nycticebus coucang*
SIZE: 15 inches (38 cm); tail 1 inch (2.5 cm)

A slow loris creeps up behind a lizard. Slowly, slowly, it inches closer and closer. Then, suddenly, the loris dashes forward and grabs the lizard with its hands. Another successful hunt!

Slow lorises are small and fuzzy, with short, thick limbs. They move slowly through the trees of the tropical forests in India and Indonesia. Hand over hand, they climb up trees to reach the fruit and tender shoots they love to eat. They spiral around tree trunks to avoid branches that stick out. They often hang upside down to eat, stretch, cool off, play, and—sometimes—to sleep.

Lorises sleep during the day, rolled up in the fork of a tree or a clump of bamboo. They wake at sundown and prepare for their night of activities. Before beginning their search for food, lorises pause to clean their fur with the long claws on their hind feet.

Hunting and eating make lorises very thirsty. They drink by touching a rain-soaked or dew-damp leaf with their fingers and then sucking off the water.

Most lorises live alone, but some roam in pairs or small family groups. A young loris stays with its mother for a whole year. Then it is ready to venture off in search of a mate.

Tarsiers

FAMILY: Tarsiidae
COMMON EXAMPLE: Western tarsier
GENUS AND SPECIES: *Tarsius bancanus*
SIZE: 5 inches (13 cm);
     tail 5 to 11 inches (13 to 28 cm)

What an acrobat! A tarsier springs backward off a tree trunk, twists around in mid-air, and lands feet first on another trunk. It clings to the tree with its extra-long tail and the sticky pads on its toes. Now it can catch that tasty insect it spied from the other tree! With a quick leap, it pounces on its prey, and grabs the victim with its hands. Dinner is served!

The tarsier is a very active primate found in the islands of Southeast Asia. Like its cousin, the loris, its sleeps during the day and roams the forest at night. With its huge round eyes, it can find fruit and insects to eat on the darkest of nights. A tarsier can also turn its ears toward a sound. This helps it find and track snakes, lizards, and small birds as they rustle about in the dark.

Tarsiers can turn their heads almost all the way around. This ability helps them spot potential victims. They can also hop on their back legs like a kangaroo or leap like a frog. Tarsiers can hop almost 24 inches (61 cm) straight up and can jump forward up to 4 feet (1.2 m) in a single leap. Insects and birds beware!

Macaques

FAMILY: Cercopithecidae
COMMON EXAMPLE: Japanese macaque
GENUS AND SPECIES: *Macaca fuscata*
SIZE: 21 inches (53 cm); tail 4 inches (10 cm)

Uh-oh, more snow! It's a good thing Japanese macaques are used to the cold. With their thick fur, these macaques can live happily in temperatures as low as 14 degrees Fahrenheit (−10 degrees Celsius).

Japanese macaques live in northern Japan, where it snows in the winter. Like humans, they have strong thumbs and can grab objects easily. They also learn quickly from each other.

Scientists gave a group of macaques sweet potatoes to see how they would react. One macaque realized that they were food and began to wash them in a nearby stream. The others caught on quickly, and soon they were all washing and then munching on the sweet potatoes.

Macaques are very social primates. They live together in groups that consist of about a dozen females and babies led by one male. At night, they sleep in treetops. In the morning, they scatter to hunt. When they are done eating, they gather together to play, rest, and groom one another.

Macaques usually have only one baby at a time. A young macaque clings to its mother's chest while she hunts, but runs around with the other youngsters during play time.

Proboscis Monkeys

FAMILY: Cercopithecidae
COMMON EXAMPLE: Proboscis monkey
GENUS AND SPECIES: *Nasalis larvatus*
SIZE: 25 inches (64 cm); tail 26 inches (66 cm)

What does "proboscis" mean, anyway? Take a good look at a male proboscis monkey and you'll find out. "Proboscis" means long, bendable nose, and that's just what a proboscis monkey has. This funny nose can be up to 4 inches (10 cm) long! The male's nose is like a loudspeaker. It makes him sound louder when he calls out to other proboscis monkeys.

These primates live in the hot, damp forests of Borneo. They live near rivers and swamps where they can find the swamp plants they like to eat. Swamp leaves are hard to digest, so their stomachs are three times as big as the stomachs of other monkeys.

They love to swim, but watch out, monkeys! A hungry crocodile may be waiting for a monkey meal.

Female proboscis monkeys and their young do not have such long, droopy noses. Their noses are smaller and turn up instead of down. Proboscis monkeys have such human faces, but look so odd, that the dark-skinned native people of Borneo call them by a name that means "white man."

Orangutans

FAMILY: Pongidae

EXAMPLE: Orangutan

GENUS AND SPECIES: *Pongo pygmaeus*

SIZE: 44 to 54 inches (112 to 137 cm)

A large male orangutan sits quietly in a tree. A female is feeding nearby. Suddenly the male hears a smaller male approaching. It inflates the throat sack under its chin like a big balloon, and gives out an earsplitting "long call."

This series of deafening groans and roars lasts about 4 minutes, and can be heard more than 1 mile (1.6 km) away. The smaller orangutan is scared, and quickly leaves the area.

Male orangutans sometimes fight each other to mate with females, but most of the time they try to avoid each other. In fact, orangutans are actually gentle, shy animals that spend most of their time alone.

At night, orangutans sleep on a platform of twigs that they have built in the fork of a tree. When the weather is cold or wet, they cover themselves with leaves to create a warm, leafy blanket. What a cozy way to spend a rainy night!

Orangutans spend their days searching for fruit, leaves, ferns, insects, and birds' eggs. They get water by licking it off leaves or scooping it out of tree holes with their hands.

Some Famous Primatologists

Wouldn't it be wonderful to live with a group of chimpanzees in the forest or watch a couple of gorillas happily grooming each other? Some scientists have done it.

They made long journeys to faraway places just to observe primates in their natural *habitats*. These scientists have learned a lot about how primates eat, sleep, and act toward each other. Scientists who study primates this closely are called *primatologists*.

One of the most famous primatologists is Jane Goodall, an Englishwoman who has spent most of her life studying chimpanzees in

Jane Goodall with a young chimpanzee

Africa. For many years, she lived in Gombe National Park in Tanzania, getting to know the chimpanzees there. After she spent a lot of time watching them from a distance, the chimpanzees began to trust her. Eventually, they let her get very close to them.

As she watched them and kept careful notes about them, she learned to identify individual chimpanzees. She gave them names, such as Flo and David Greybeard, and made notes about their different personalities.

In 1965, Jane founded the Gombe Stream Research Center, so other primatologists could come there to study chimpanzees. In 1976, the Jane Goodall Institute for Wildlife Research, Education, and Conservation

Chimpanzee group observed by Jane Goodall

was founded to make sure that these studies would continue.

Another scientist with a love of primates is John MacKinnon, an Englishman who has studied apes all over the world. He began studying with Jane Goodall in Gombe and has since been to Asia and all over Africa. He has observed gibbons, chimpanzees, gorillas, and orangutans. He spent many years living closely with these primates and has written several books that explain what he has learned about them.

John believes that humans and apes are very similar. He has watched gorillas and orangutans make sleeping nests, just as humans make beds. He has also observed chimpanzees create and use tools.

Dian Fossey
with young
gorillas

According to him, groups of apes are a lot like communities of humans. They have similar types of rules and family ties.

Dian Fossey was another famous primatologist. She spent 13 years studying mountain gorillas in the Virunga Mountains of Africa. Like Jane Goodall, she earned the trust of the gorillas she studied. They even allowed her to live among them, as though she were a mountain gorilla, too!

One of Dian's main goals was to protect the gorillas from poachers—people who kill animals illegally and sell their body parts. She let the world know that mountain gorillas are in danger and helped get laws passed to protect the lives of these gentle primates.

Perhaps, one day, you will decide to become a primatologist and help the rest of the world learn more about our fascinating primate cousins.

Words to Know

class—a group of creatures within a phylum that share certain characteristics.

family—a group of creatures within an order that share certain characteristics.

genus (plural **genera**)—a group of creatures within a family that share certain characteristics.

habitat—the environment where a plant or animal lives and grows.

hyoid bone—a bone at the base of the tongue.

kingdom—one of the five divisions into which all living things are placed: the animal kingdom, the plant kingdom, the fungus kingdom, the moneran kingdom, and the protist kingdom.

order—a group of organisms within a class that share certain characteristics.

phylum (plural **phyla**)—a group of creatures within a kingdom that share certain characteristics.

prehensile tail—a tail that can be used for grabbing and grasping.

primatologist—a scientist who studies primates.

species—a group of organisms within a genus that share certain characteristics. Members of a species can mate and produce young.

3-D vision—the ability to see objects in three dimensions.

troop—a group of primates that hunt, eat, and sleep together.

Learning More

Books

Goodall, Jane. *My Life with the Chimpanzees*. New York: Pocket Books, 1996.

Lovett, Sarah. *Extremely Weird Primates*. Santa Fe: John Muir Publications, 1996.

Maynard, Thane. *Primates: Apes, Monkeys, Prosimians*. New York: Franklin Watts, 1994.

Saign, Geoffrey. *The Great Apes*. Danbury, CT: Franklin Watts, 1998.

Videos

Among the Wild Chimpanzees. National Geographic Videos.

Gorilla. National Geographic Videos.

Tales of the Snow Monkey. Lorne Greene's New Wilderness Series.

Web Sites

Monkey Madness provides information about primates in captivity. **http://www.monkeymadness.com.**

Tiso shows painting of primates created by the artist Tiso. **http://members.aol.com/artprimate/tiso.html.**

Primate Gallery allows you to watch animated sequences of primates, listen to primate calls, view a list of living primates, and see photos of many primates. The site features a primate of the week. **http://www.selu.com/~bio/PrimateGallery.**

Index

About the Author

Erin Pembrey Swan studied animal behavior, literature, and early childhood education at Hampshire College in Massachusetts. She also studied literature and history at the University College Galway in Ireland. Her poetry has been published in two volumes of *The Poet's Gallery* in Woodstock, New York, and in *The Cuirt Journal* in Galway. Although Ms. Swan lives in New Paltz, New York, she spends a great deal of time traveling to different parts of the world.